DRIVING HOME

DRIVING HOME

DAVID AGAR JAICKS

Special thanks to Jeanne Peck, Mr. lei,
Melissa & Jessika from The Troy Book Makers,
and to all the librarians who have helped me along the way.

To order additional copies of this title, contact your favorite
local bookstore or visit www.tbmbooks.com

Cover and book design by Melissa Mykal Batalin

Printed in the United States of America
The Troy Book Makers • www.thetroybookmakers.com

ISBN: 978-1-935534-105

To Mom,
and Babbie, our second Mom, and good friend

Contents

UNDER THE INFLUENCE

SPEEDING ALONG

ENGINE TROUBLE

PARALLEL PARKING

UNDER THE INFLUENCE

Chicago

Papers, leaves, and garbage
spin in the wind
like sharks feeding
in the open courtyard.

An old abandoned Cadillac
sits low in the street
wheel hub sunk in asphalt
black rubber lifted
beneath the wheel wells,
chrome dimpled with rust
Seeds from Elm trees drifted
in piles
like dry cereal across the hood.

A woman walks out of the alley
arm tight up under the purse
lips alive with lipstick
high heels talking
upon the pavement.

She moves off into the blue
artery of the city.
Alone on the street are cars and trees
and squirrels.

Ice Storm

The tree

branches

are encased

in test tubes

of ice

as Willy

and I

walk the

unknown forest.

June

From across town came boys on bicycles; screaming, yelping, lifting up onto their rear wheels and riding for fifty yards.

"Pop a wheely!"

They met other boys behind the DQ, riding no-handed, riding one-handed, eating ice cream cones and swarming through the cars like bees.

"C'mon!"

They passed the bakery and the grove of cigar trees with their narrow, twisting pods. They cut behind Art's Garage, over the greasy gravel, and passed the trunks of wild radiator hoses snorkeling up through the grass.

"Watch out!"

They passed the Instant Car Wash, its lathered brushes whirling, its men posed like bull fighters, ready with rags. Then the path stole north into the forest and the boys disappeared, leaving only spruce boughs waving and dust to settle upon the weeds.

Driving

There's Dane.

He Drives a truck

for State Line Potato

Chips.

I pass white pine,

fences,

old barns doing

yoga in the snow.

Mom

At night the puppy and I

lay out on our backs

on the lawn

and look up at the stars.

There is a circle of trees

and the moon

seems to go around

like a big can opener

opening up the sky.

where I poke my long nose

up through to heaven

and I swear I can smell

my Mom up there, as usual,

she is at her stove, cooking.

Last night she made

brownies. I remember how good

they were.

Night before she made her

stroganoff. I remember how the

noodles coiled around like the long

doormats the janitors would

kick to the side when they swept out

the hallways of my grade school.

I remember how she drove me there

every day, even when the Chicago snows were

quite tall. I remember walking into those

hallways, stomping my boots, and how the world

seemed so fresh and clean in the morning.

Eventually the stars

begin to glitter like sugar,

and of course

I am not tall enough yet

to reach her,

and taste those wonderful brownies again.

Later, we roll onto our stomachs

and walk inside.

The house can seem

so lonely and dark

when we return.

DAVID AGAR JAICKS

Oil Stains

Sitting back like an astronaut

I look up into a light that shines

like the shell of an oyster.

I see Carla

my dental hygienist

appear on the horizon

of my mouth.

She is wrapped in gear

and her small tool is singing

like a chainsaw

only from many octaves

away.

She is the only one

I know

who can work

in pajamas

and get

away with it.

Later, walking out,

I pass small rooms

where people are

lying about

and think back to a time

perhaps during the Civil War

when patients struggled

and the doctor

lurched from those rooms,

exasperated,

his chest red with blood

the way oil stains

a piece of

cardboard.

Still Life

Sunlight with

bright yellow

covering the trees

Each leaf

feeling the weight

of the wind

Shade patterns

with green

and yellow

Summer air rises

in sugar maples

like a dream.

Picnic at the Johnson's

I remember eating hot dogs and baked beans and how the paper plates would turn gray where the baked bean juice soaked through. I remember watching the Beatles on TV for the first time, in black and white, on the Ed Sullivan Show. My friend was already a drummer and my dad had said, "Those guys need haircuts." I didn't feel that way then but now I'm not so sure.

I remember the feeble attempts at a volleyball game in the backyard. The ball would volley once or twice over the net then go skidding sideways off the hand of someone's big sister. Then one of us would have to pick carefully through the poison ivy to retrieve it from the woods.

I remember the dogs, of course. The Collies with their dense fur pack and long pointed noses like camp saws.

And I remember sitting on the edge of the picnic bench at the end of the night, next to my mom, pinching and flopping the loose skin on the backside of her arm while she talked. It reminded me of turkey skin and I called it her gobbler.

She still managed to smile, though with a little sadness locked inside.

Kitty

Her boa

a red vine

climbing

the tree

of her neck.

Her legs

candles,

waxy

and smooth.

Her

face

shining,

Her hair

grassy

as

a willow.

The Road Curled

The other day I drove to work
the road curved with smiles
the hills rolled
and squirreled
the earth
laughed and swung

I lent to time
as I drove
and drove
on and on
home.

Two Old Friends

This takes place five or so years from now and Willy, my dog, and I are walking down a snowy, plowed road, the same type of road I walked him on when I first took him out as a pup and the plowed sides kept him with me on the road. Only now he can talk, and he is asking me questions about the world and what people generally understand, and what he has always wanted to know.

"The rain falls onto the earth, collects in rivers that flow into the sea, and the sea water evaporates into the sky and eventually falls as rain onto the earth. That's the hydrologic cycle, basically."

We walk on for awhile. Off to our side a high tree branch loses its snow.

"What did your Dad do?" he asks.

"He was a pilot in the Second World War and he worked as a salesman most of his life."

I bend down over and continue to say, "I didn't know your Dad but I bet he was as handsome as you are."

We continue to walk. Suddenly he stops, turns and looks up at me.

"Why do they call them Milkbones?" he asks.

"I don't know, but I've been wondering that for a long, long time," I reply.

Tonight

The moon is big

round and full

and swims backstroke

among the stars.

SPEEDING ALONG

Migrant Woman

A cliff

her face told

her hair wind spoken

and as she tried to stand

even the setting sun

couldn't show her the way

couldn't keep its head

above the horizon.

Fireflies

When I was a child, in summer, in Illinois, my parents
would put me to bed and I would watch the orange
tea bag sun drool its light among the willows, hear the
thunder of timbers as a car went over the bridge, and the
sound of a lawn mower from someone cutting their lawn
far off would die away to nothing.

San Francisco

At night
lying down
looking sideways
out of my uncle's window,
I see low flying airplanes
going so slowly across the sky.
They seem to be hanging and sparkling
like Christmas ornaments
in the evergreen
in my uncle's
backyard. What
splendor they
have here!

Pushing Forty Five

Pushing midway

into forty five

I stop and lift

up my shirt

My stomach rolls out

like the hump

of a grave

or a rolling hill

in the suburbs.

a good place

for houses

with land

going up.

I smooth my belly

and let it rest.

If I am lying on

my side

all bellys are created equal.

If I am standing,

I have won out.

In a speaking contest

of no words

just soft

white skin.

Cody

My dog

knows no A-bomb, H-bomb

he sleeps

and dreams of rabbits

in tall grass

and porcupine sun

he wanders through field birds

high under a low fence

all in a round summer

his pink tongue long

and fluttering,

he stands in the open creek

and drinks

his mouth cutting the current

down river

his tail made thinner by the water

he shakes off

just close enough

to make me run:

bright water in a wreath

off his collar,

his white face

clear as sun

his old wood eyes

always shining.

Driving East

In winter
the vineyards
of western Pennsylvania
are entangled
brown and wiry
arms over shoulders,
chorus girls
dancing in a
line.

Fireworks

First a pounding thud as a trailer goes up into the sky.

It waggles its way like a tadpole trying to escape into the mud, or a hammer being thrown way up high.

For a moment it disappears, turning its back on us.

Then there is a boom and a spider of colors weeds out above our town.

The ground is awash in light.

I stop thinking about women or the fool I've been tonight dancing in front of the band.

I stand amazed as though I am seeing the birth of the universe.

How many people see this, I wonder, in Uganda, or Peru, or poorest India, or Iran?

I don't notice my back against a fencepost, a piling in the harbor of this parking lot at the bank.

I only see the garden of fire above me and then the crowd laying back with their paint roller faces, big and flat and oval, and covered with light.

At the Fairgrounds

Clouds
like buffalos
nudge their heads
eastward

a chocolate chip cookie
of birds
rises and falls
in heavy wind

a square from
a tin roof
lifts like the
gills of a dying fish

and

no horses rode
this summer,
dry goldenrod and
milkweed stems

stand
in families
beside the empty
cinder track.

Mountain River

There is a river
back in my home
that falls
through the mountains.
Whitewater
roaring through
narrow granite chutes,
like baskets of flowers,
or long flowing hair,
spilling over cascades
where it
smooths out
and goes winding
off into the valley.
Spreading
over the farm land.
When it's high,
reaching for the sea.
Gently turning
at big bends
and crossed
by bridges
that carry trucks and cars
and people
going sideways
across its path.

The Carpenters

When I was forty-nine I became a carpenter. I took a walk down the road with my dog, turned up a mud driveway where there was a house going up, and got a job.

The next morning I arrived for work. It was January, and we had a propane stove that fired all day inside where we would occasionally gather like homeless men and hold out our hands and rock back and forth in front of the flames.

Since it was winter, I was prepared. I always wore my stretchy long underwear to work. But throughout the day, as I went often from upstairs to downstairs, or outside to inside, the underwear would begin to descend from my back down my butt. By the end of the day, I always knew it was time to go home because it would be angled as low as it could go.

It was like my own internal sundial. At noon I could pretty much tell it was time to break for lunch because it would be halfway down my butt.

The top of the house was beautiful, I remember those early days. We hadn't gotten quite all the rafters up and it was a full view of one side of a valley and we were up in the tops of trees.

One day I was alone on the upper floor, working, and the house was vibrating. Kevin, a full fledged carpenter, was using the Sawzall on something downstairs. A Sawzall, in case you didn't know, is a long, powerful electric tool like a swordfish with a blade coming out of its nose.

All of a sudden I heard a yelp, and the saw and house were quiet.

Kevin had sawed into his hand.

When a carpenter hurts his hand like that it's something you remember.

Noah called up from down below and said very calmly, "Dave, I'm taking Kevin to the hospital."

The two of them walked off down that mud driveway to a truck and drove away, Kevin's hand raised, red with blood and glistening like a cranberry.

I stood there in silence for a while on top of that house among a cathedral of rafters and sun and thought this I will always remember.

ENGINE TROUBLE

Clara

A friend realized suddenly he didn't want trees around him, he wanted people and buildings. So he moved to New York.

His move seemed revelatory, like when you are sitting in your living room, looking around, and suddenly you realize that chair belongs in the corner, not your mother's sofa.

Now, Clara, his four year old golden retriever is living with Willy and I. She balances Willy's dark amber with her lighter maple syrup gold.

She is also as wide as a bench. Occasionally I will see her out of the periphery of my vision, and think, gosh, I'd like to sit down. But I'm sure she'd move way from me like a floating kickboard.

Often while we are out on a country road and Willy is fielding a jumping tennis ball, Clara likes to be on her back, legs splayed, writhing into the snow pack as if she were skydiving backwards into the center of the earth.

Later, her heavy stance will remind me of a sheep, gazing at us square on through gentle, smiling eyes.

Cinema

Almost alone in the movie theater,

the soles of my shoes

merging with coca cola

and bits of popcorn.

The floor is

unexplored terrain.

I am sitting in the back.

Cold air hits my neck.

Down in front, a girl stands.

She looks up at seats

that are mostly empty.

I look back at her.

We balance

the distance

like we are

on a teeter-totter.

From There to Here

I had to go to the hospital the other day for a stress test. Too much had accumulated on the shore.

I lay down, watched the ceiling, thinking of my heart beating or not beating, life and death, and when to pick up the dog.

A nursing team flew about like the Marx brothers, complete with open lab coats, jumping eye brows, and looking at me from upside down.

I felt light headed, started to see a gold fish swimming in the clear plastic I.V. bag floating above my head.

I was reminded of my childhood. My friend and I would ride our balloon tire bikes to our school fair in the summer.

We loved the whole thing—the butterfly collections and handwriting contests—but best of it was trying to win a gold fish by throwing a ping pong ball into one of the mouths of fifty glass jars where inside each one rested a sleepy elegant gold fish.

Oh, our hearts were beating then like big hurried caterpillars, or wind through parachutes that were downed.

If we got lucky we rode home fast with a fish in a clear plastic bag clenched against our handle bars.

I would like to thank my heart for its service this long.

I'd like to at least take it out to dinner and a movie. I'd like to thank it for getting me up all those hills, and over all those bumpy girlfriends, and over all those bumpy girlfriends getting over me. For continuing when all those police cars appeared in my rear view mirror. For the bartenders, school teachers, therapists, and former employers who are now starting to come forward, lining up for their chance at the microphone inside me.

But mostly, I'd like to ask its forgiveness for my own mother's heart that decided to rest during the long Bataan-like march of my adolescence, and then refused to go on.

JW Construction

I am working upside down
removing old tract lighting
from the ceiling

the boss tells me to cut
the wires and wrap them
with tape.

I cut each one and
turn them into thin
black mummies.

Than I stuff them into
their little silver
sarcophagus above my
head.

We go on.

Dog Nation

It's amazing sometimes how you learn how some things are made. The sofa arms on my sofa were stuffed with soft white cotton. Now, when I come home during the day, it is as if I am flying in an airplane high above the earth and looking down on a lovely partly cloudy sky. Soft white puffs of cotton are lofting above my hardwood floors.

I am at war with my eight month Labrador Retriever.

The nights and days are a constant power struggle over the territories of the house. At night, I usually control the upper floor, but if I take a moment to brush my teeth or clip at an unwanted hair, I may have lost a shoe or a favorite necktie, or a corner on my piano may now be rounded.

I must be alert and aware at all moments.

The lower floor, where most of the battles are fought, now resembles the barren landscapes of France between the trenches during the First World War.

There is no lone charred and blasted tree twisting up through the mustard gas and fog, only an electric fan oscillating eerily like a search light, blowing the cotton and bits of torn fabric into the corners. And the screen in the window, where he tried to get at some workmen, flies like a shredded flag.

Working Woman

She rises early

wearing her basement

face.

Makeup adorns

her white skin.

Heavy pollen on a tiger lily,

or on the

thorax of a bee.

The Rolling Land

The rolling land

in the horizon,

the proud shade

dawn is

early sun.

People step high

people step low

on the leaves

in the rain.

Returning

Here I am again on an airplane heading home, looking down on the sky which resembles a vast pond of ice with patches of clouds like snow drifting across its surface.

I think back to Bridon's pond where we played ice hockey as kids. My mom used to say it was really just the effluent from the Bridon's family septic system and she didn't understand why it could freeze. I guess, thinking back, it was really sort of a big popsicle of shit.

Anyway, for us, it was a grand rink located in the hollowed gown of a willow.

I remember red cheeks, bent ankles from loosely tied laces, and lots and lots of fun. The puck often got lost inside the legs of our dogs. And a little brother of someone might spend part of the game on all fours because my Springer Spaniel had him gripped in a sex act which neither the little brother, nor I, fully understood.

At the end of the day the sun ripened. We slung our skates over our shouldered sticks, and headed home, true tired champions of the neighborhood, walking over roots like frozen knuckles on a path shining with ice, our heals inside our socks glistening with new blisters.

Hardware Store

Cheryl and I are standing at the duplicate key machine as she attempts to make me a key. The little grinding wheel starts to ring like the loose chain on a mini-bike.

Half jokingly I say, "It's like raising a kid. You fit the first key in, tighten down, and then next key comes out exactly the same."

"How many kids do you have?" she says looking over at me.

"Zero," I say and make fingers into an O.

She leans over and locks eyebrows with me.

"It's not like raising a kid," she says.

As I walk out, I have trouble fitting my money back into my wallet.

War

They came out of the Washington suburbs

to watch the battle of Bull Run.

Men and women finely dressed

standing on a hillside

like a Christmas tree farm

some taller than others

but all stood planted

as the blue smoke

from the musket balls

settled in the treed valley below.

The soldiers fought like they would

never fight again.

PARALLEL PARKING

Bill's Party

Tonight I sat
we all sat
and spoke
and laughed
and watched the moon
sit down like a man
with a beer belly
smother his chair

in the late evening
among the ringing crickets.

Each voice
clogging the night

My mind as dense as a sofa.

The young sprang about
with hula hoops
circling them
like little Saturns
the ghosts of the party.

All of us in planetary motion
out on the lawn
all fitting in.

Ugly Morning

It's early
I'm shaving
my face looks like a coconut
cream pie
the sun is drooping
the neighbor's dog
has a cough
I walk outside
rediscover my car
under snow

smooth as a
melted candle

the way night
merges into day.

Stripping a Roof at Dominick's

Drip Edge, otherwise known as Dave, stands below the second story as pieces of shingle are thrown down and land, slapping flat onto the tarp covered earth. Old flashing that is crinkled falls like giant pieces of nachos. Black tar, like cheese, is dripped across the silver surface.

It is lunchtime. Dominick's tree, planted on September 11, is weeping out like an ornamental cedar. Private planes take off and fly overhead from the Salt Creek airport. Willy, my dog, is curled like a fox and hibernating in the back of my Toyota.

We finally break and I drive away, turn onto Rt. 47 and eventually begin to pass above the farm along the Split Tree River. I start to think of a friend of mine who may never get out of here before her life begins.

I look down at the blonde corn rows marching along the river, and wonder if we choose the channels our tears flow through like the small rivers that slowly cut deeper and deeper into the ground. I look up river and wonder where it all started.

I'll never know, I think, and let my sadness happen as Willy and I drive on into the town.

The Fans

In summer the doors of the house open like eyes as the house wakes up. My puppy goes in and out through the shade curtains. When it is hot and humid, we all lie stagnant, the breath of the fans covering our bodies.

One fan seems to be telling us a story, its round face rotates back and forth in an airy conversation, keeping perfect eye contact with everyone in the room and giving each of us an exact measure of attention as we lie under blankets of humidity, surrendering from our battles with late July.

This fan reminds me of a proper woman visiting. She is rather stout and sits upright, talking to us. She needs to talk. It is her role. She is not a good listener at this moment.

I guess that is what winter is for, a time for our fans to listen.

She is like a teacher or an explorer who spent the entire winter trekking through the attic of my house, rappelling rafters, and camping among the empty suitcases and boxes of old family photos, while I was asleep in the next bedroom. And now, in late summer, she wants to tell us about it. It's okay. I like what she has to say.

I wonder what she'll do this winter, I think, when I pack her away. Maybe she'll dive with fishes off a reef in my basement where the water can get quite tall. And when the next summer rolls around, I hope she'll be quite excited to tell us about it.

First Meeting

After they removed their hats,

her hair

fell down

around her

head

in a chandelier

of brown

ringlets.

His hair

was matted.

A deer

had slept

in the grass.

Together they moved

tired, forward

into the

secret forest,

lifted by the warmth of their smiles.

Swim Practice

Fingers interlocked

arms outstretched

back stroking

battle ships

heading out

into open

ocean.

Later, as coach

gives talk in corner,

they are like feeding fish,

happily diving

and surfacing the water.

Willy

The puppy and I go to sleep at night sharing the same mattress. Part of the night he lays on his back with his legs splayed out. He is a raft on a blue ocean.

Somewhere in the night we lie back to back like two men about to duel each other. Couldn't you see us march off one pace and try and blast each other off the corners of the mattress? We'd probably miss and go back to sleeping back to back while pieces of drywall hinged by the wallpaper dangled around us.

Sometimes when he is dreaming he lays with his legs over the edge, his paws twitching and bending gently like fishing poles when the fish are biting.

And me, I go about finding my dreams like laying leaves on a turning river.

Summer

After chasing the tennis ball

for a good long hour

Willy sits down

inside the ribcage of a fern,

his pink tongue long

and fluttering.

Where it is Sweet and Fancy

Tina works as an ice cream technician:
her hips swaying round and round
as she draws vanilla
soft serve
into a paper bowl.

Her cheeks are like
scoops of ice cream
sprinkled with freckles
that are fading
with time
like stars
at early dawn.

Monument Mountain

Sometimes while driving home
I'll see a great shoehorn in the sky.

Sometimes while driving home
I'll see a cloth of clouds
polishing over that shoehorn,
the tops of that high bluff and rock,
as if it were getting a good shine.

Sometimes while driving home
I will remember
how I polished my dad's shoes
when I was a child.

He paid fifteen cents a shoe.
I thought it was a good deal
then and I still do now.

He even adjusted for inflation.
I got a nickel more every year,
and then it became a dime.

Then sometimes I'll be driving home
and think
how the mountain and the man
have become the same.

The author wishes to thank the following magazines and periodicals for earlier publications:

"Driving" appeared in *The Haight Ashbury Literary Journal*

"Oil Stains" appeared in *Fence Magazine*

"Dog Nation" appeared in *Passages North,* and was awarded Honorable Mention prize in the *Thomas Hrushka Memorial Nonfiction Contest*